DANGER BELOW!

NEEDLES OF PAIN!

STONEFISH ATTACK

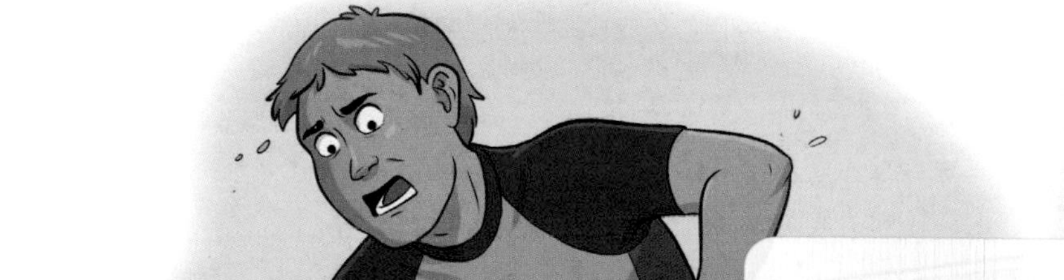

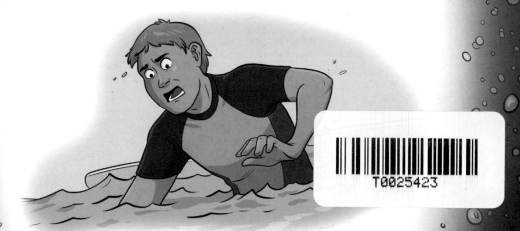

BY JAMES BUCKLEY JR.

ILLUSTRATED BY CASSIE ANDERSON

BEARPORT PUBLISHING

Minneapolis, Minnesota

BEAR CLAW

Credits

20T: © Lim Tiaw Leong/Shutterstock; 20B: © Vladimir Wrangel/Shutterstock; 21: © RGB Ventures/ Superstock/Alamy; 22T: © Vitaliy6447/Shutterstock; 22B: © Ruslan.Salikhov/Shutterstock.

Produced by Shoreline Publishing Group LLC
Santa Barbara, California
Designer: Patty Kelley
Editorial Director: James Buckley Jr.

DISCLAIMER: This graphic story is a dramatization based on true events. It is intended to give the reader a sense of the narrative rather than a presentation of actual details as they occurred.

Library of Congress Cataloging-in-Publication Data

Names: Buckley, James, Jr., 1963– author. | Anderson, Cassie, illustrator.
Title: Needles of pain! : stonefish attack / by James Buckley Jr. ;
    illustrated by Cassie Anderson.
Description: Bear claw edition. | Minneapolis, Minnesota : Bearport
    Publishing, [2021] | Series: Danger below! | Includes bibliographical
    references and index.
Identifiers: LCCN 2020008624 (print) | LCCN 2020008625 (ebook) | ISBN
    9781647470548 (library binding) | ISBN 9781647470616 (paperback) | ISBN
    9781647470685 (ebook)
Subjects: LCSH: Stonefishes—Juvenile literature. | Stonefishes—Comic
    books, strips, etc. | Graphic novels.
Classification: LCC QL638.S42 B83 2021 (print) | LCC QL638.S42 (ebook) |
    DDC 597/.68—dc23
LC record available at https://lccn.loc.gov/2020008624
LC ebook record available at https://lccn.loc.gov/2020008625

For more information, write to Bearport Publishing, 5357 Penn Avenue South, Minneapolis, MN 55419. Printed in the United States of America.

Contents

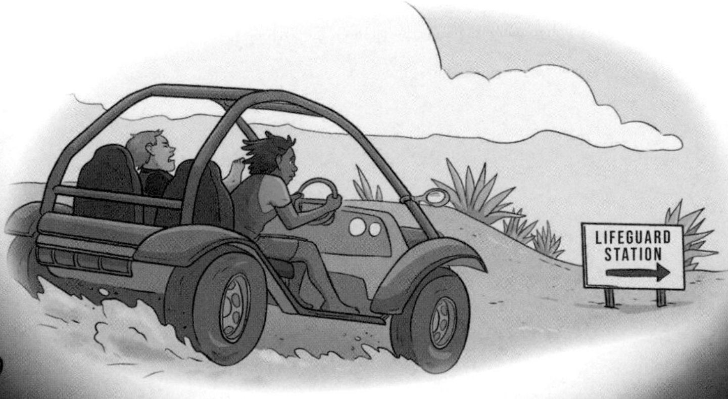

LIFEGUARD STATION

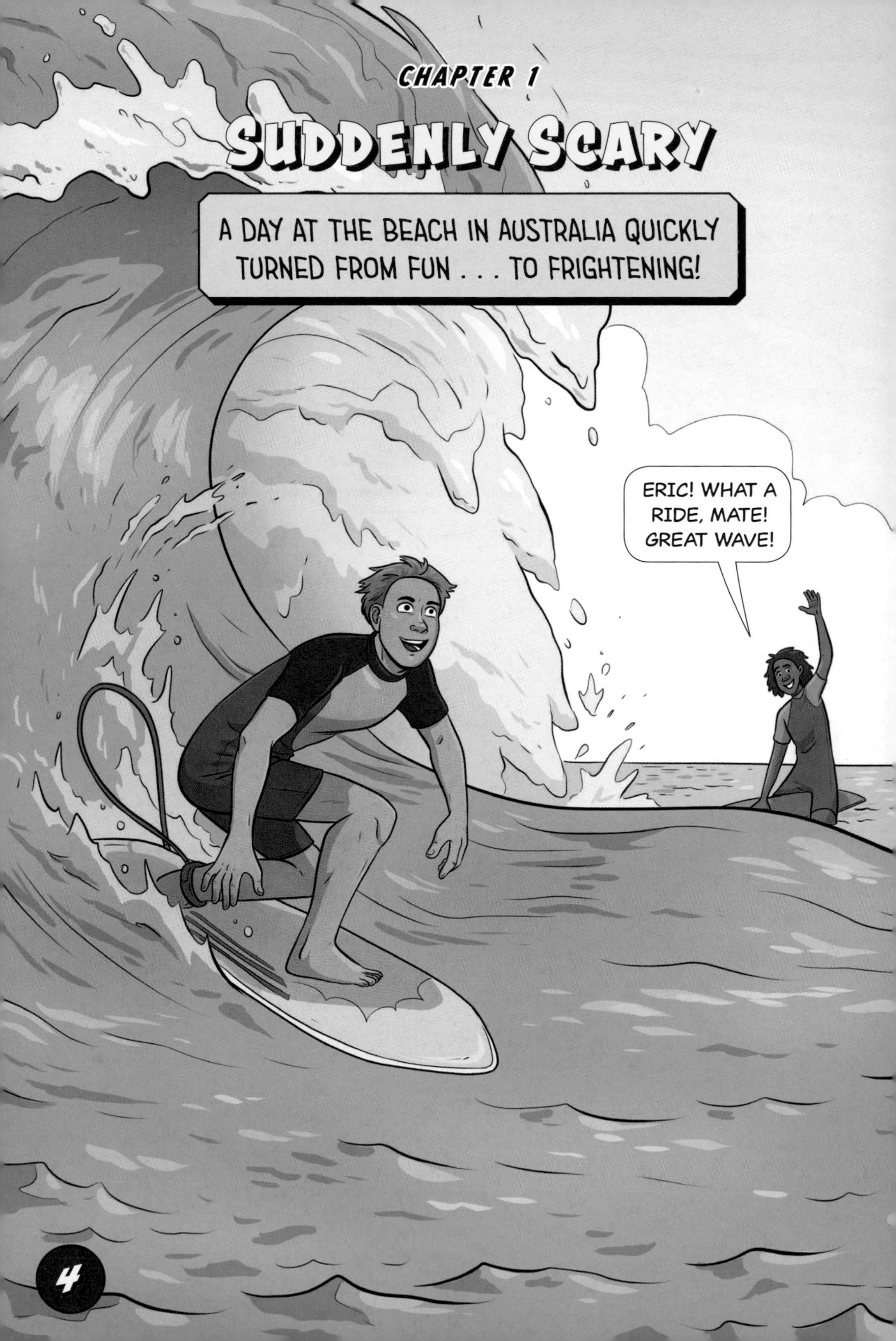
CHAPTER 1
SUDDENLY SCARY
A DAY AT THE BEACH IN AUSTRALIA QUICKLY TURNED FROM FUN . . . TO FRIGHTENING!
ERIC! WHAT A RIDE, MATE! GREAT WAVE!

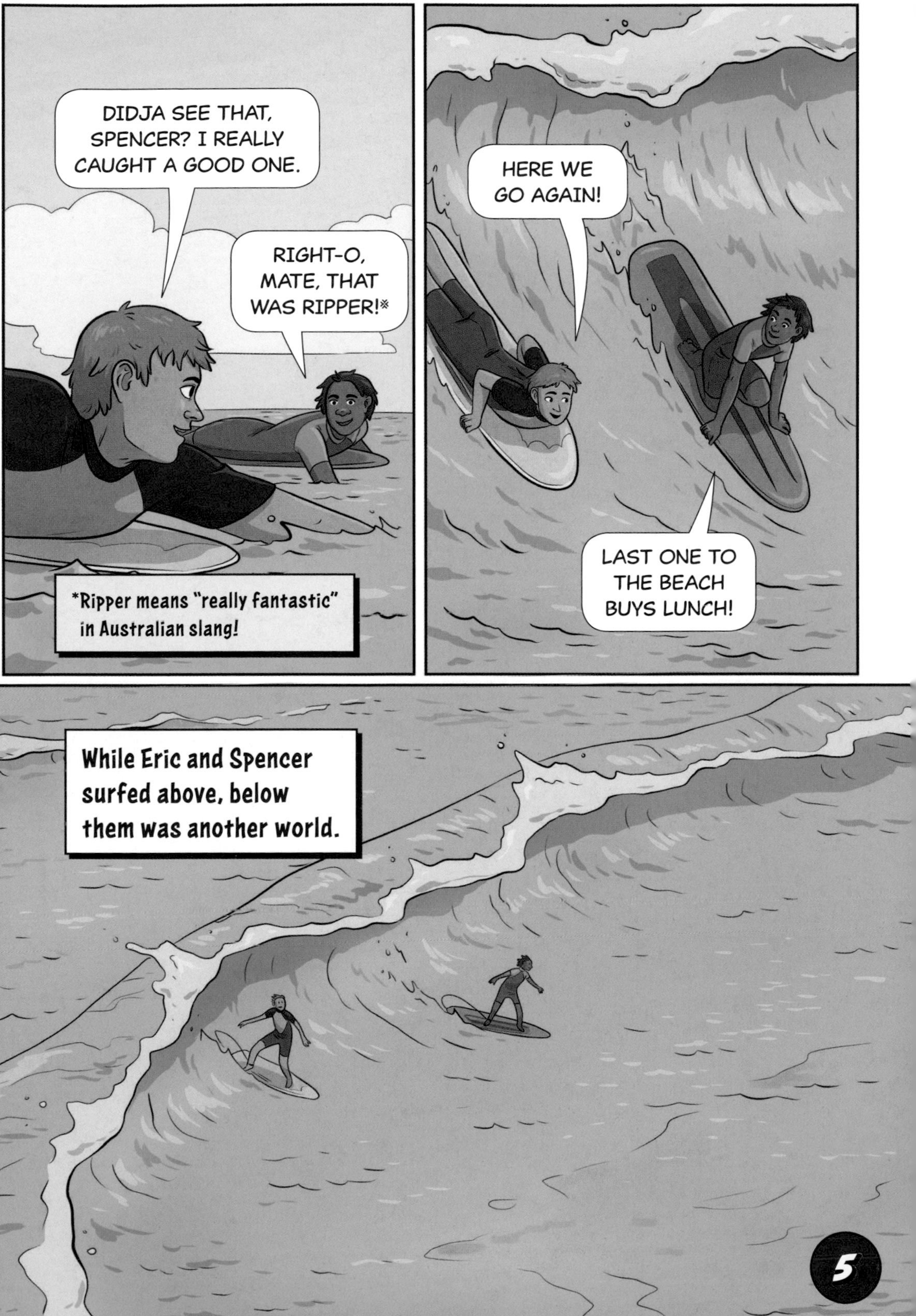
DIDJA SEE THAT, SPENCER? I REALLY CAUGHT A GOOD ONE.
RIGHT-O, MATE, THAT WAS RIPPER!*
*Ripper means "really fantastic" in Australian slang!
HERE WE GO AGAIN!
LAST ONE TO THE BEACH BUYS LUNCH!
While Eric and Spencer surfed above, below them was another world.

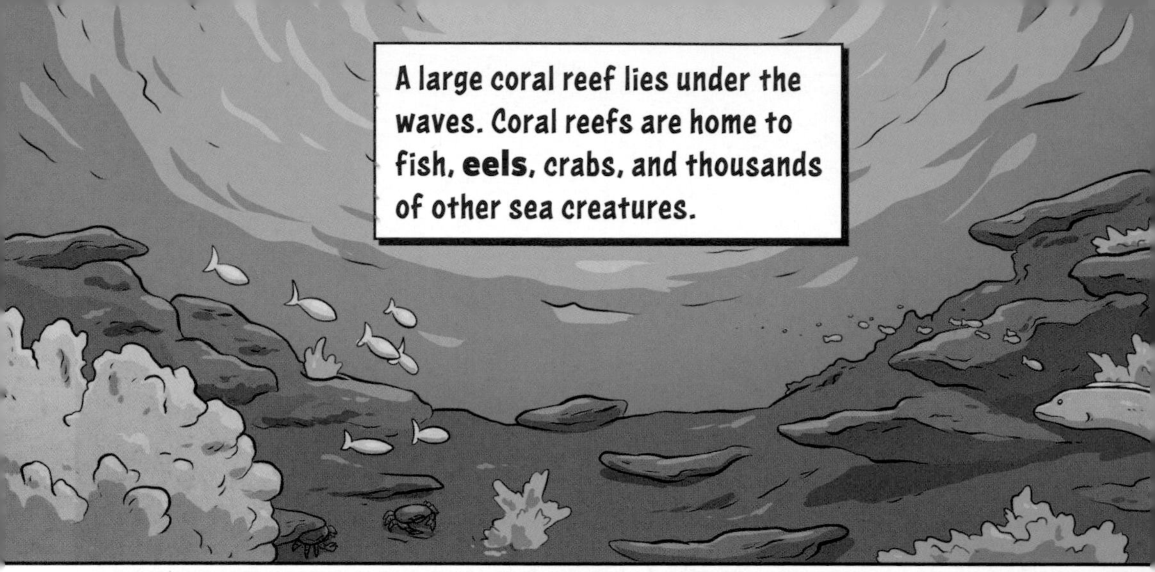
A large coral reef lies under the waves. Coral reefs are home to fish, eels, crabs, and thousands of other sea creatures.

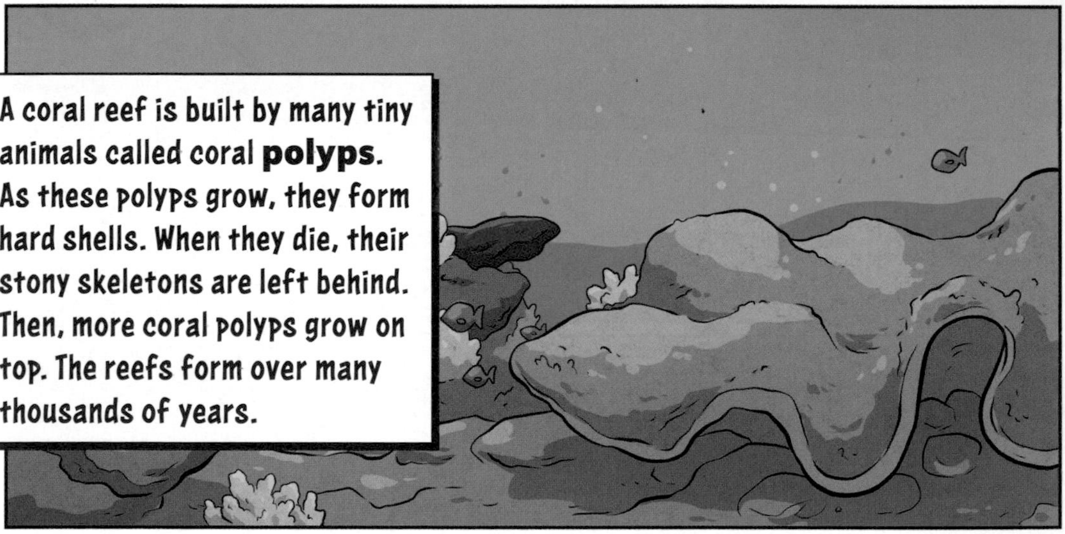
A coral reef is built by many tiny animals called coral polyps. As these polyps grow, they form hard shells. When they die, their stony skeletons are left behind. Then, more coral polyps grow on top. The reefs form over many thousands of years.

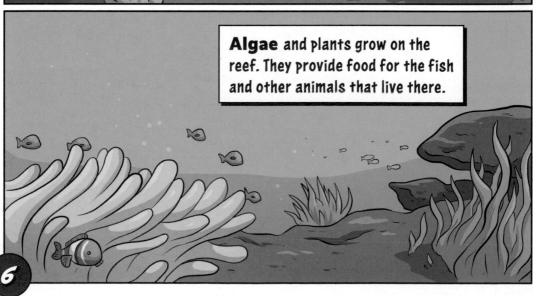

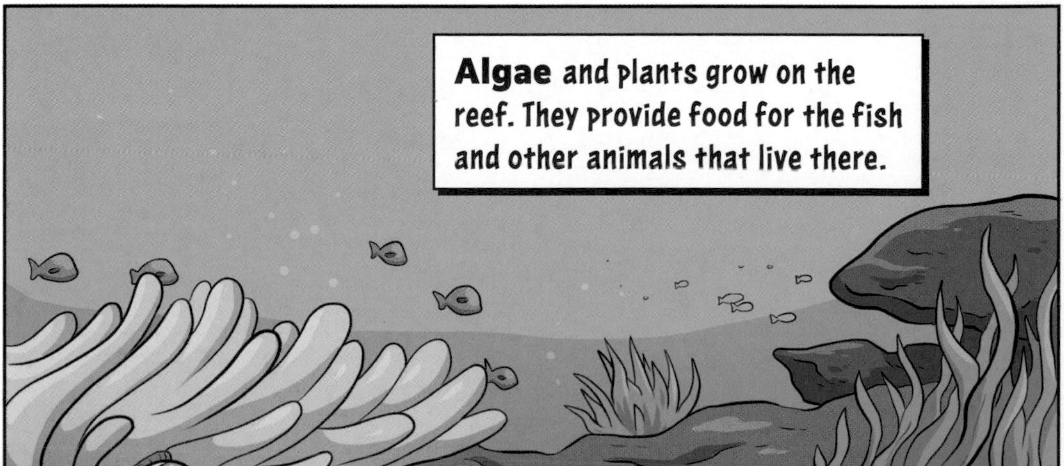
Algae and plants grow on the reef. They provide food for the fish and other animals that live there.

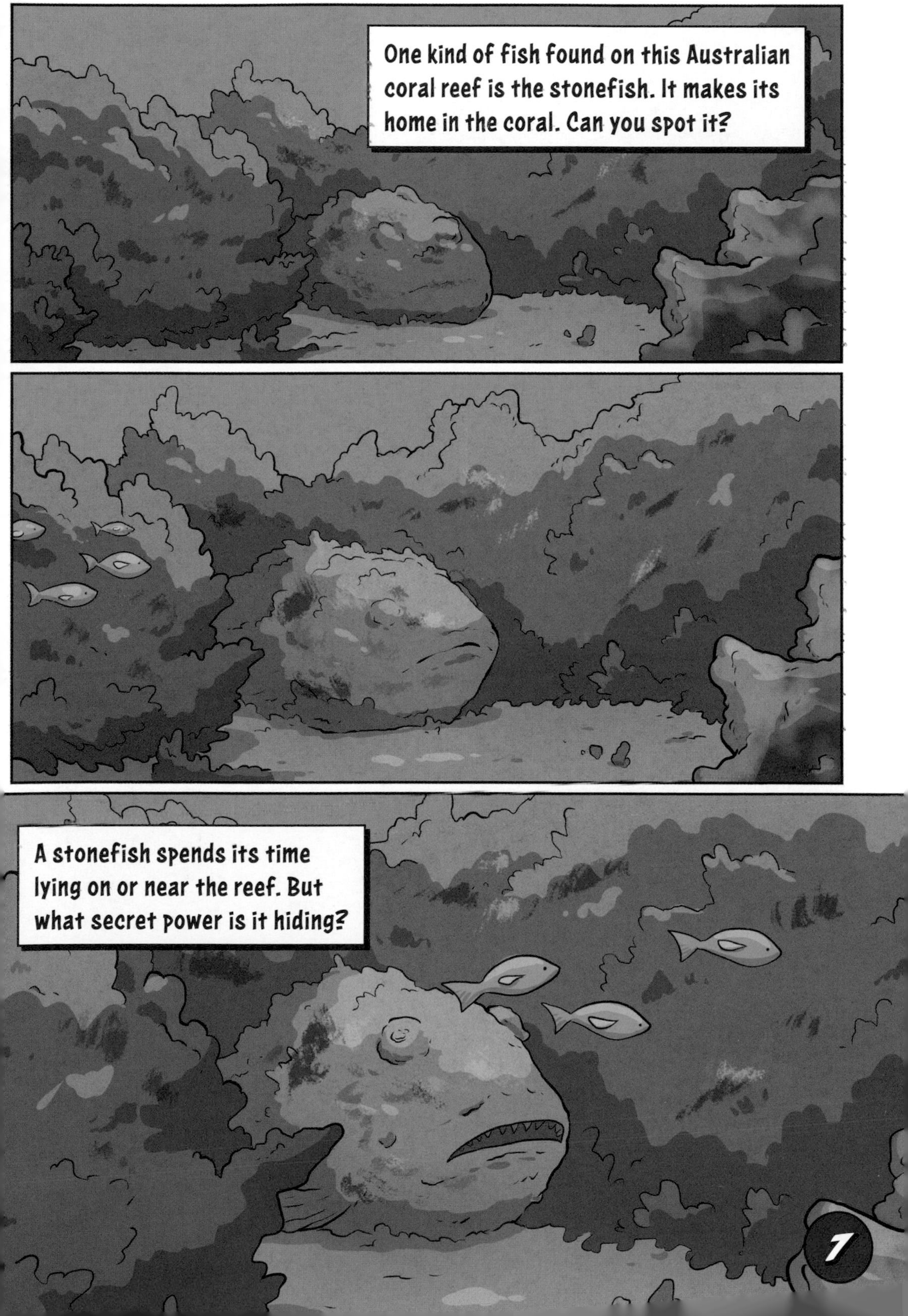
One kind of fish found on this Australian coral reef is the stonefish. It makes its home in the coral. Can you spot it?
A stonefish spends its time lying on or near the reef. But what secret power is it hiding?

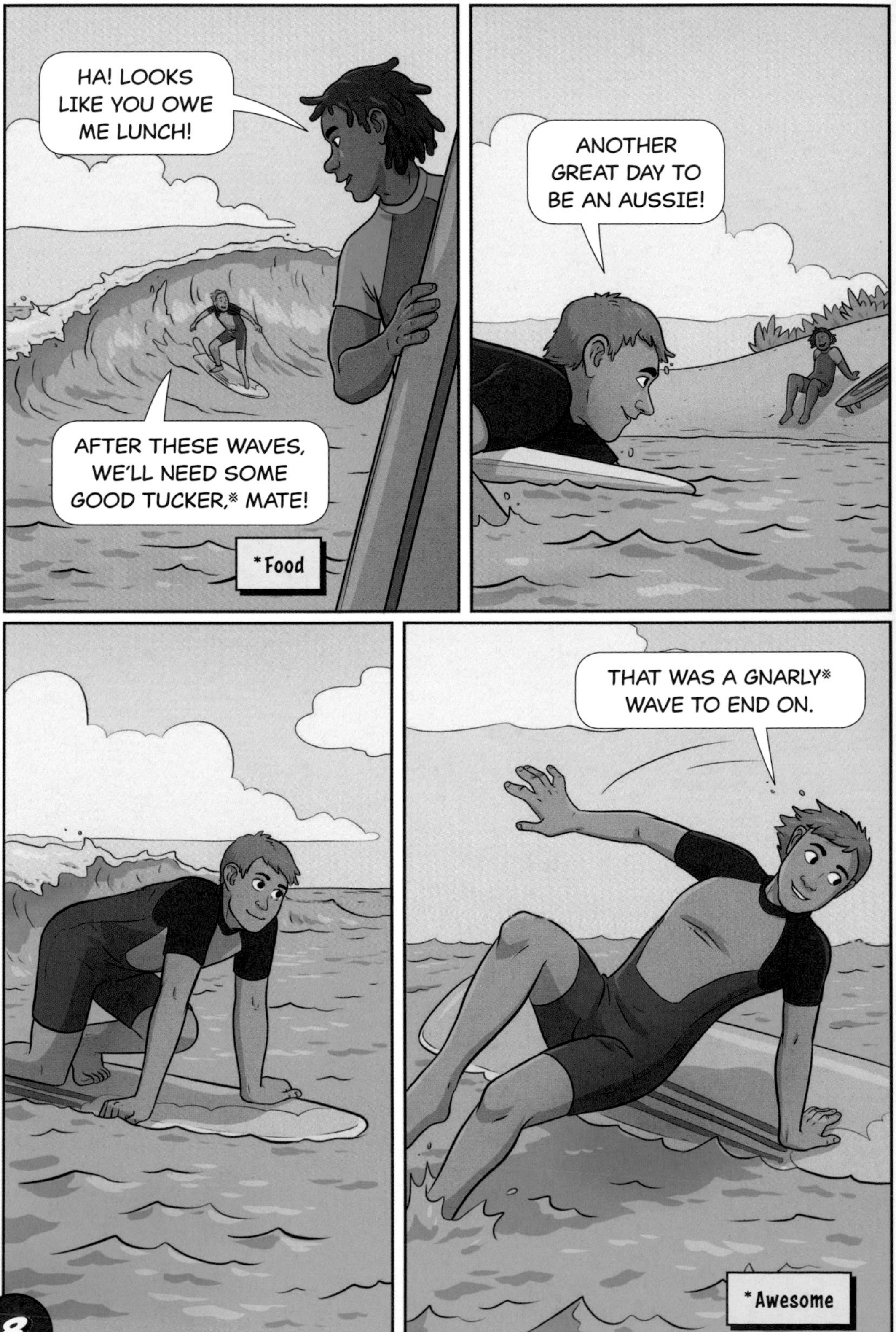
HA! LOOKS LIKE YOU OWE ME LUNCH!
AFTER THESE WAVES, WE'LL NEED SOME GOOD TUCKER,* MATE!
*Food
ANOTHER GREAT DAY TO BE AN AUSSIE!
THAT WAS A GNARLY* WAVE TO END ON.
*Awesome

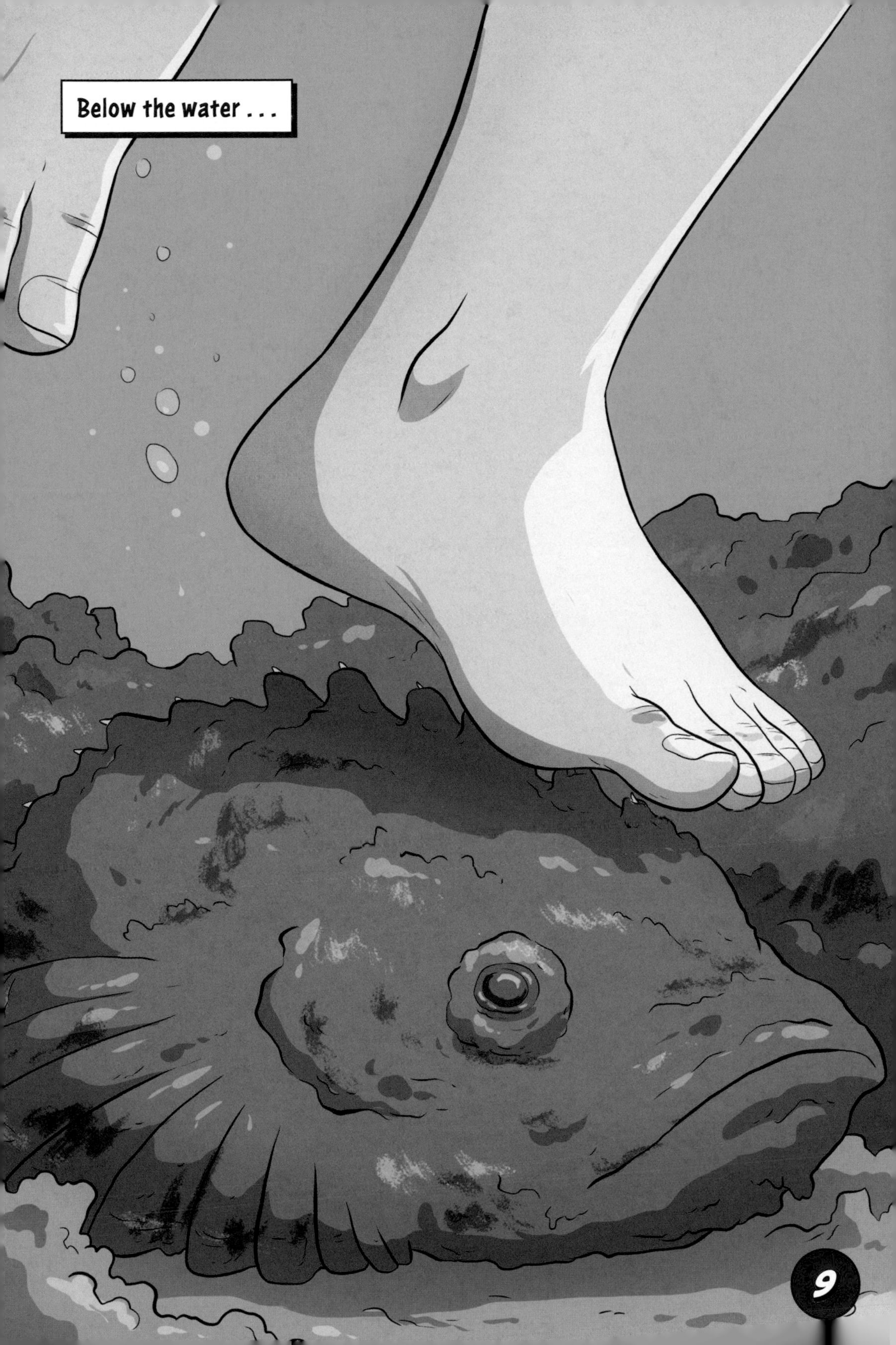
Below the water . . .

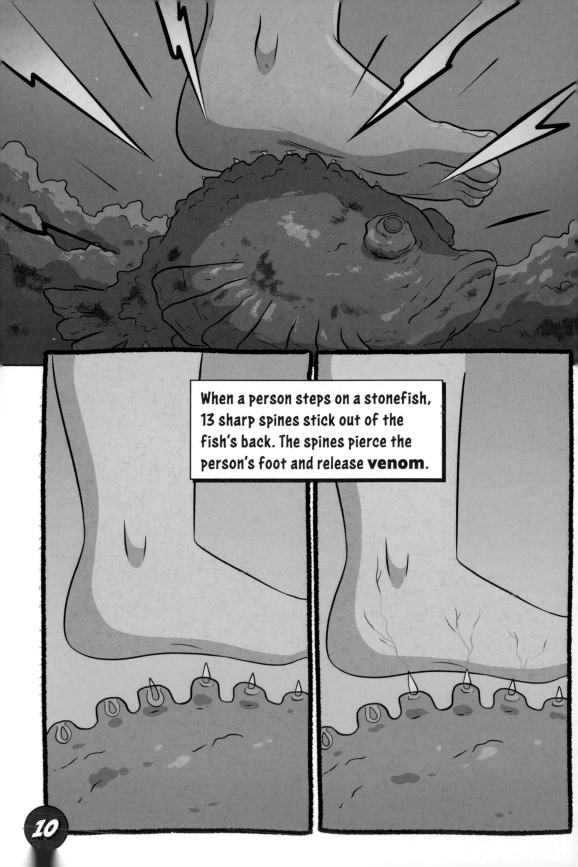

When a person steps on a stonefish, 13 sharp spines stick out of the fish's back. The spines pierce the person's foot and release **venom**.

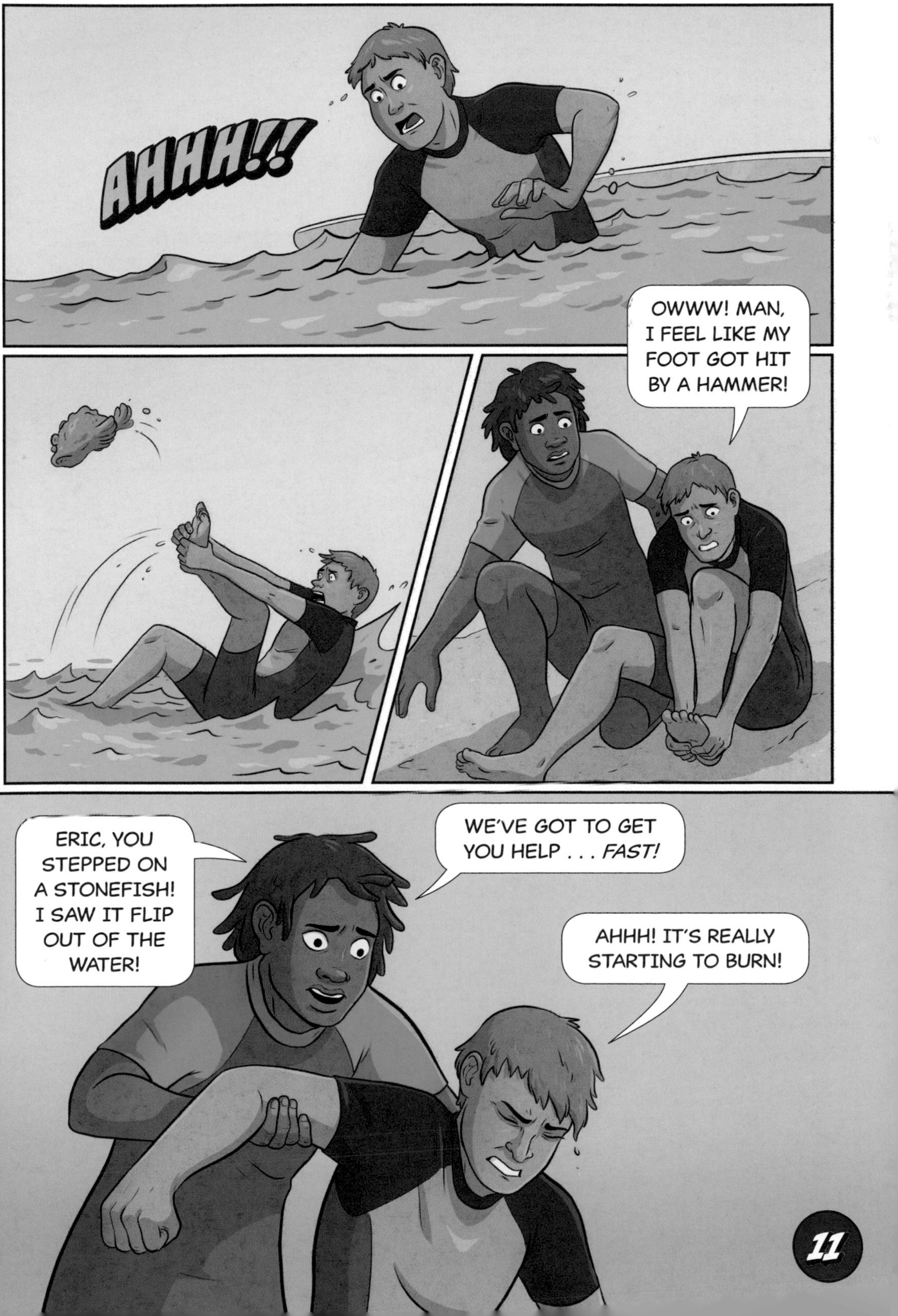
AHHH!?!
OWWW! MAN, I FEEL LIKE MY FOOT GOT HIT BY A HAMMER!
ERIC, YOU STEPPED ON A STONEFISH! I SAW IT FLIP OUT OF THE WATER!
WE'VE GOT TO GET YOU HELP . . . *FAST!*
AHHH! IT'S REALLY STARTING TO BURN!

CHAPTER 2

TO THE RESCUE!

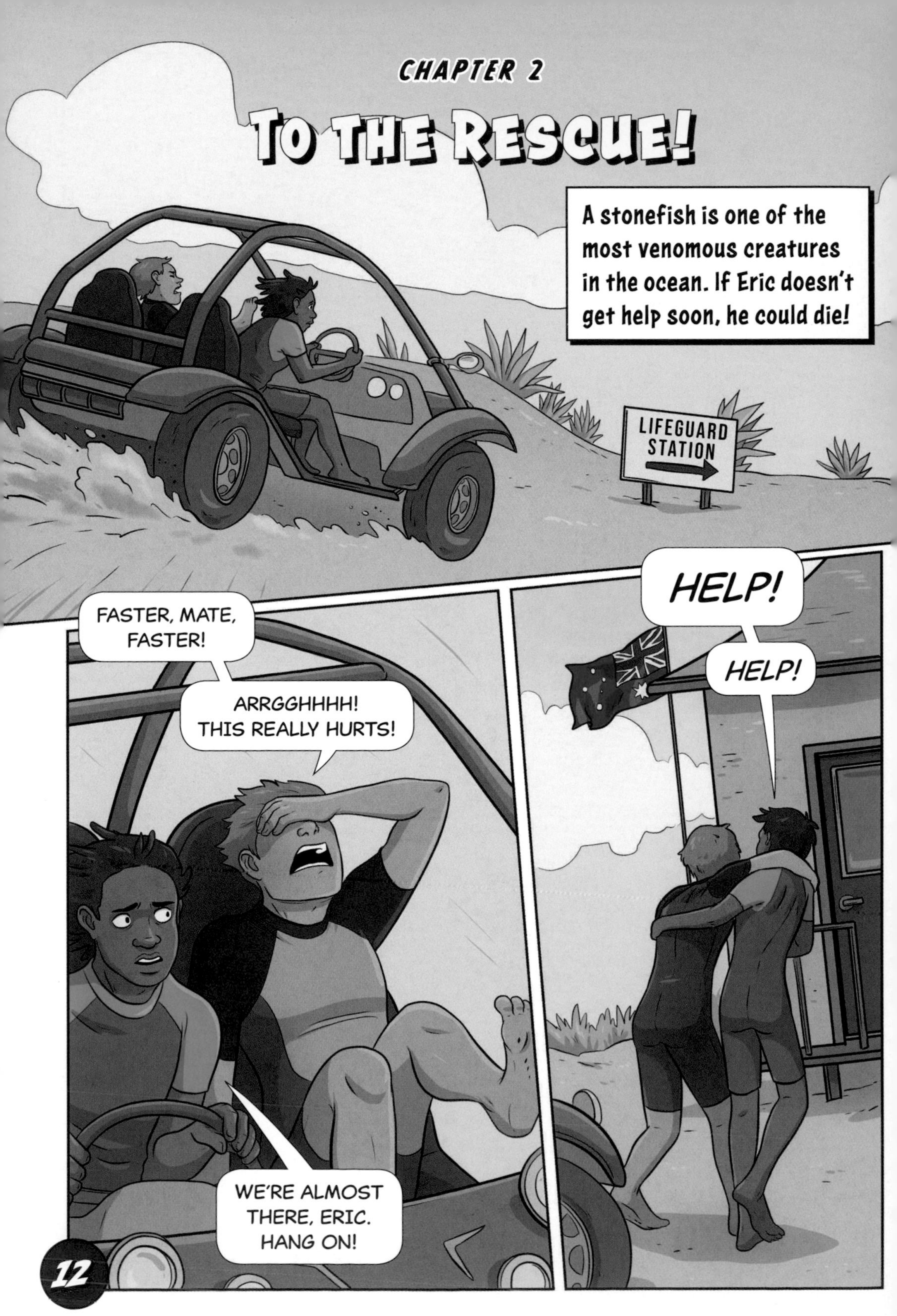
A stonefish is one of the most venomous creatures in the ocean. If Eric doesn't get help soon, he could die!
LIFEGUARD STATION
FASTER, MATE, FASTER!
ARRGGHHHH! THIS REALLY HURTS!
WE'RE ALMOST THERE, ERIC. HANG ON!
HELP!
HELP!

MY MATE ERIC HAS BEEN STUNG BY A STONEFISH!

HE NEEDS HELP!

RIGHT, SIT HERE. WHEN DID THIS HAPPEN?

JUST A FEW MINUTES AGO. HURRY!

OKAY. LET ME GET WHAT WE NEED.

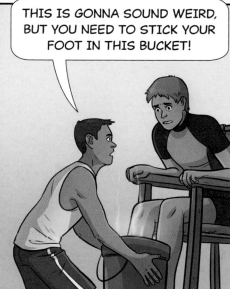

THIS IS GONNA SOUND WEIRD, BUT YOU NEED TO STICK YOUR FOOT IN THIS BUCKET!

WHAT?!

TRUST ME, MATE! I KNOW WHAT I'M TALKIN' ABOUT!

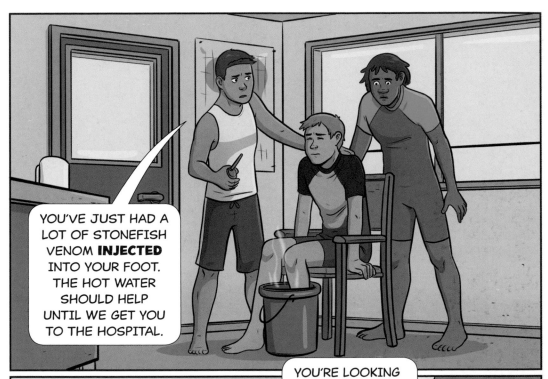

YOU'VE JUST HAD A LOT OF STONEFISH VENOM **INJECTED** INTO YOUR FOOT. THE HOT WATER SHOULD HELP UNTIL WE GET YOU TO THE HOSPITAL.

I'VE ALREADY CALLED THE AMBULANCE AND THE HOSPITAL. THEY'LL HAVE THE **ANTIVENIN** WAITING FOR YOU.

YOU'RE LOOKING A LITTLE PALE FROM THE PAIN. LET'S GET YOU SOMETHING ELSE.

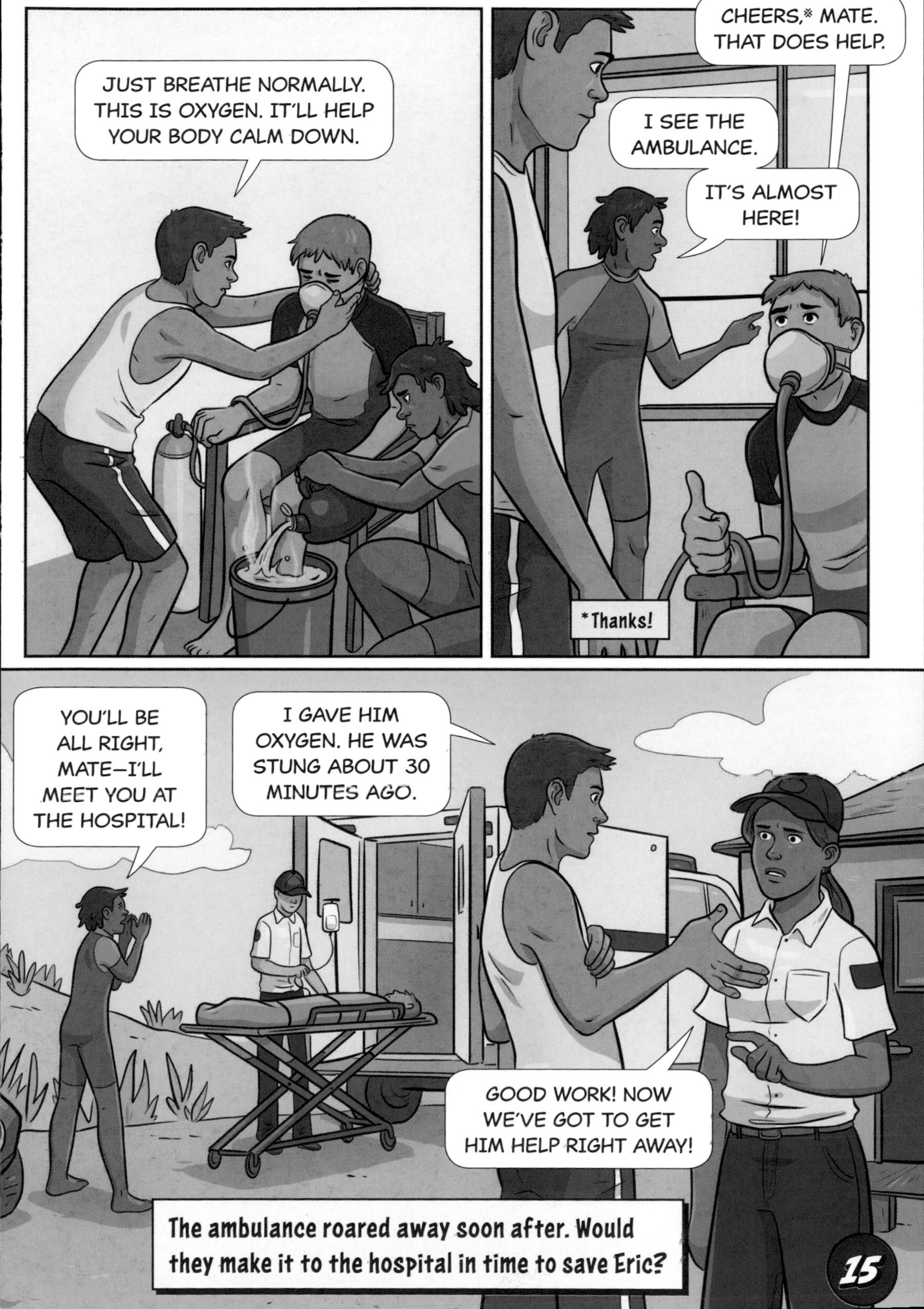
JUST BREATHE NORMALLY. THIS IS OXYGEN. IT'LL HELP YOUR BODY CALM DOWN.
CHEERS,* MATE. THAT DOES HELP.
I SEE THE AMBULANCE.
IT'S ALMOST HERE!
*Thanks!
YOU'LL BE ALL RIGHT, MATE—I'LL MEET YOU AT THE HOSPITAL!
I GAVE HIM OXYGEN. HE WAS STUNG ABOUT 30 MINUTES AGO.
GOOD WORK! NOW WE'VE GOT TO GET HIM HELP RIGHT AWAY!
The ambulance roared away soon after. Would they make it to the hospital in time to save Eric?

CHAPTER 3

A Close Call

HERE'S THE STONEFISH VICTIM.

HE HAS AN **ELEVATED** HEART RATE, AND HE'S GETTING OXYGEN. HE NEEDS THE ANTIVENIN RIGHT AWAY!

WE'VE GOT IT! BRING HIM IN.

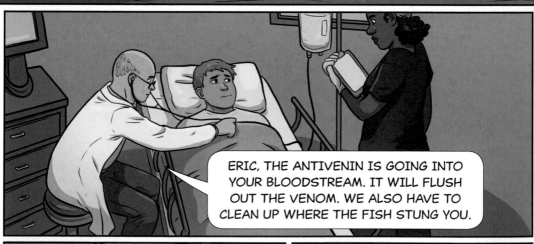

ERIC, THE ANTIVENIN IS GOING INTO YOUR BLOODSTREAM. IT WILL FLUSH OUT THE VENOM. WE ALSO HAVE TO CLEAN UP WHERE THE FISH STUNG YOU.

WE'LL MAKE SURE NONE OF THE STONEFISH SPINES GOT STUCK IN THERE.

HMM . . . I DON'T SEE ANY, BUT WE'LL TAKE A CLOSE LOOK.

PLEASE TAKE A *VERY* CLOSE LOOK.

I DON'T WANT TO TAKE HOME ANY SOUVENIRS FROM *THIS* BEACH TRIP!

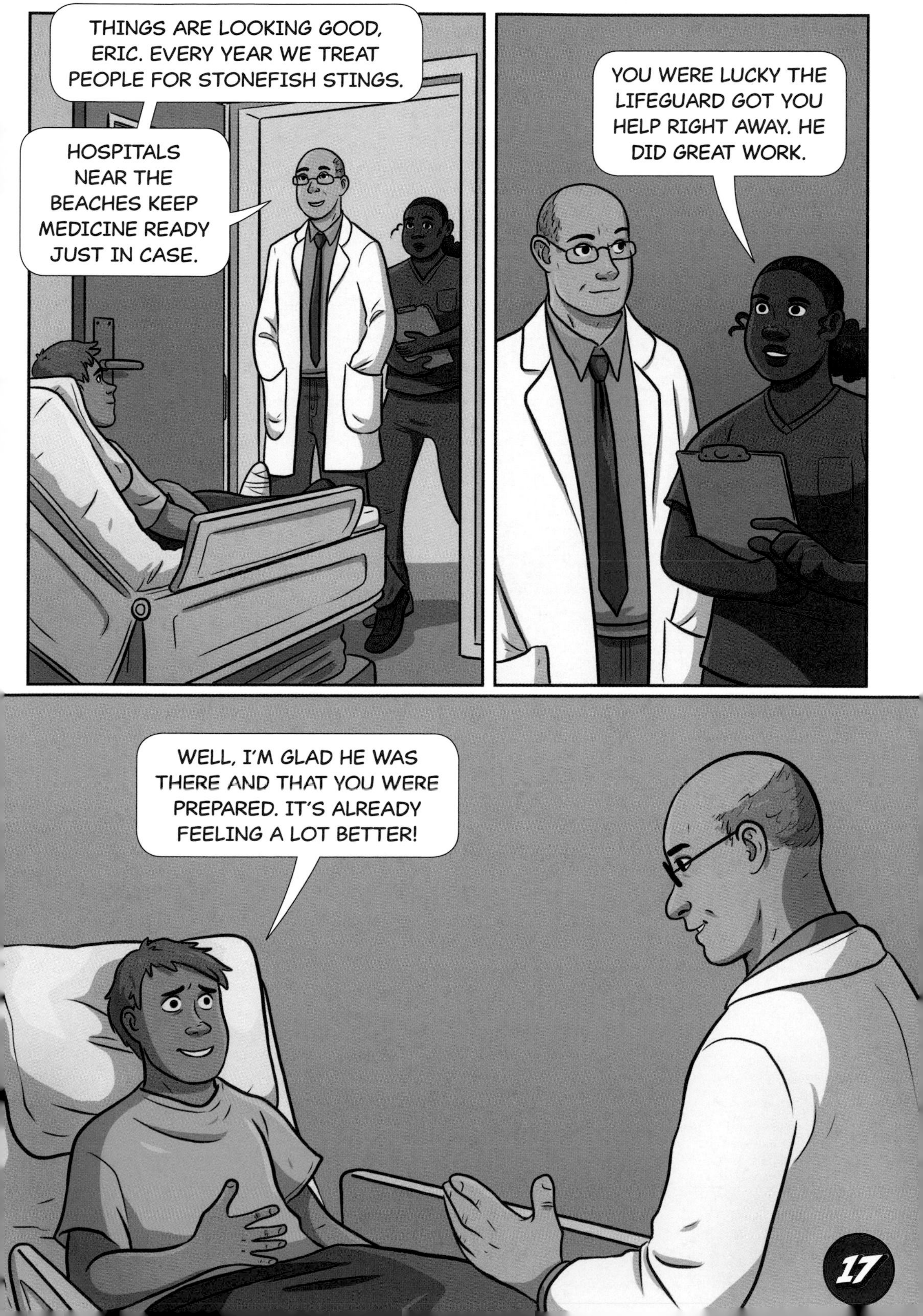
THINGS ARE LOOKING GOOD, ERIC. EVERY YEAR WE TREAT PEOPLE FOR STONEFISH STINGS.
HOSPITALS NEAR THE BEACHES KEEP MEDICINE READY JUST IN CASE.
YOU WERE LUCKY THE LIFEGUARD GOT YOU HELP RIGHT AWAY. HE DID GREAT WORK.
WELL, I'M GLAD HE WAS THERE AND THAT YOU WERE PREPARED. IT'S ALREADY FEELING A LOT BETTER!

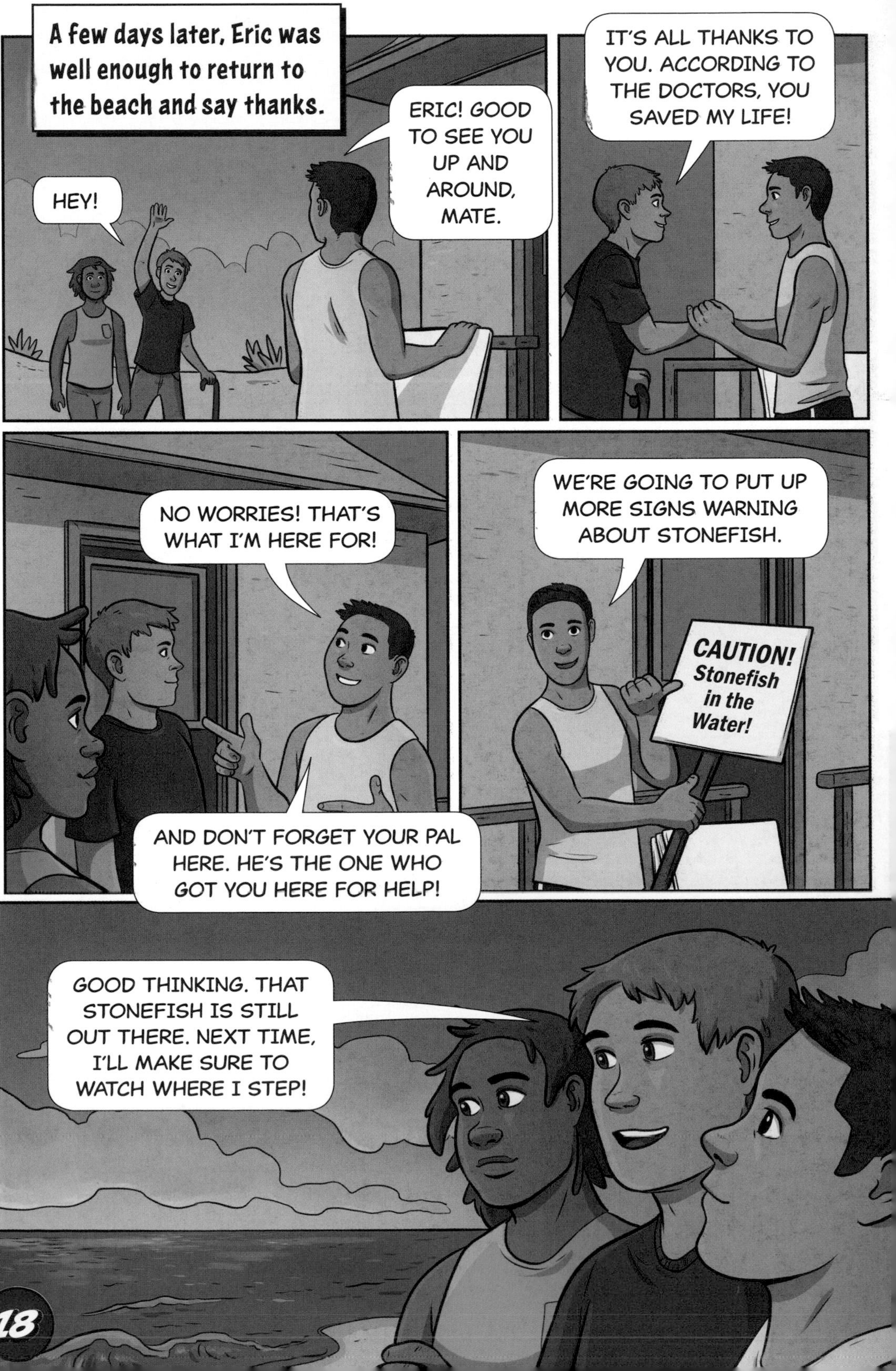
A few days later, Eric was well enough to return to the beach and say thanks.
HEY!
ERIC! GOOD TO SEE YOU UP AND AROUND, MATE.
IT'S ALL THANKS TO YOU. ACCORDING TO THE DOCTORS, YOU SAVED MY LIFE!
NO WORRIES! THAT'S WHAT I'M HERE FOR!
AND DON'T FORGET YOUR PAL HERE. HE'S THE ONE WHO GOT YOU HERE FOR HELP!
WE'RE GOING TO PUT UP MORE SIGNS WARNING ABOUT STONEFISH.
CAUTION! Stonefish in the Water!
GOOD THINKING. THAT STONEFISH IS STILL OUT THERE. NEXT TIME, I'LL MAKE SURE TO WATCH WHERE I STEP!

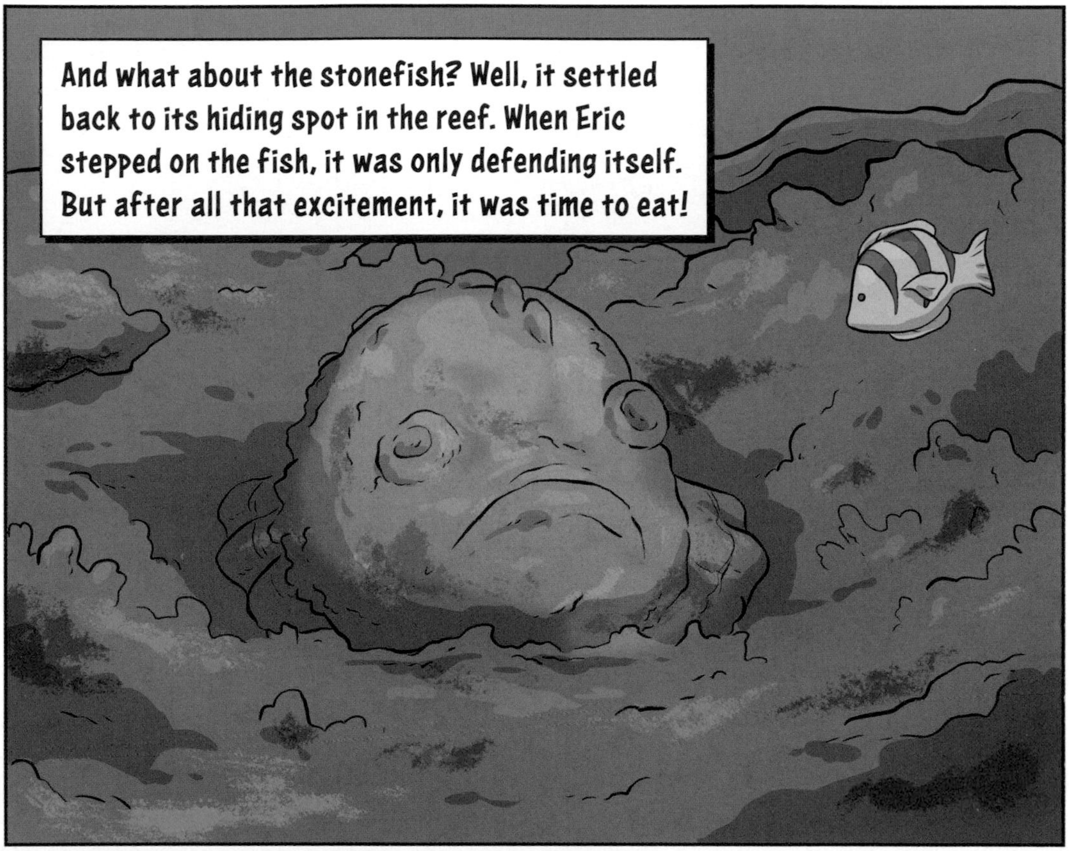
And what about the stonefish? Well, it settled back to its hiding spot in the reef. When Eric stepped on the fish, it was only defending itself. But after all that excitement, it was time to eat!

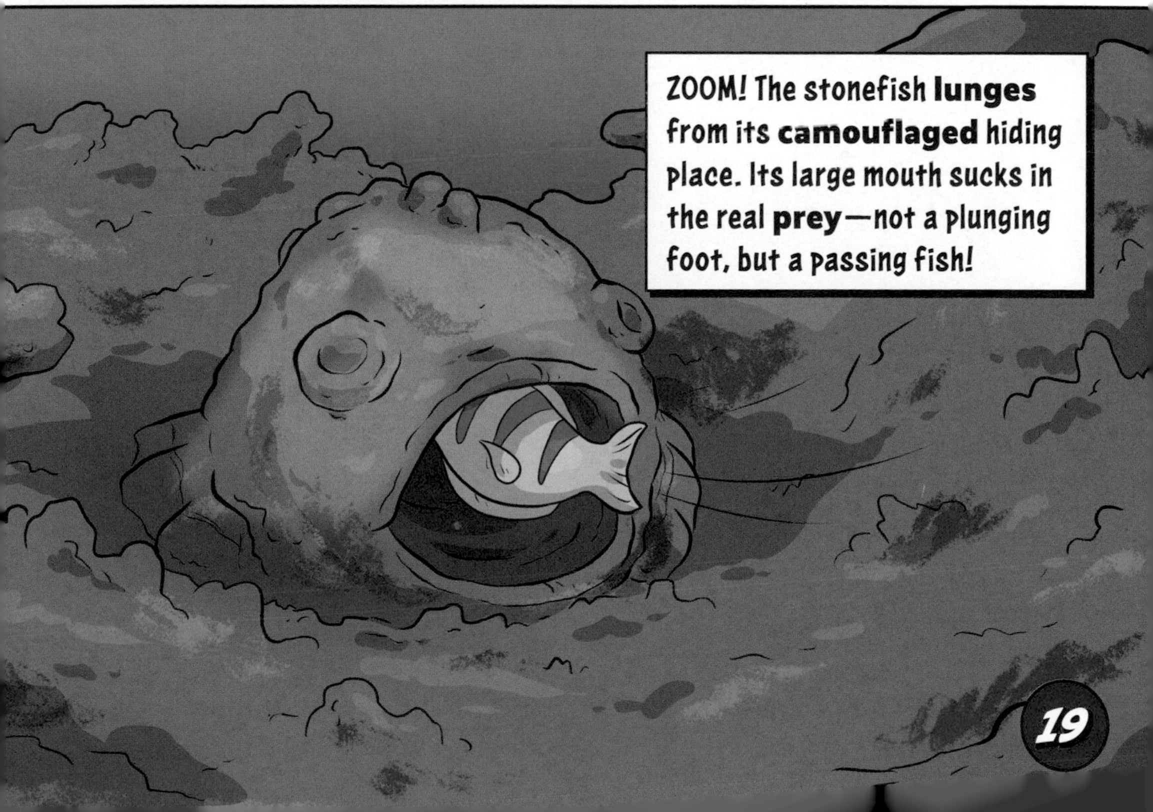
ZOOM! The stonefish **lunges** from its **camouflaged** hiding place. Its large mouth sucks in the real **prey**—not a plunging foot, but a passing fish!

About Stonefish

There are more than 30 different species of stonefish—all with toxic spines. These spines are used only for defense. The skin and scales of these fish help them blend in with the reefs where they live. To catch food, a stonefish lies still and waits for shrimp or small fish to swim by. Then, it quickly opens its mouth, sucks in the prey, and swallows it whole.

Stonefish

- Each stonefish spine has enough venom to kill about 1,000 mice.

- A dead stonefish can still pass venom to someone who steps on it.

- A stonefish can chomp down on its prey in about a tenth of a second!

- Most stonefish live in warm waters in the Indian and southern Pacific Oceans.

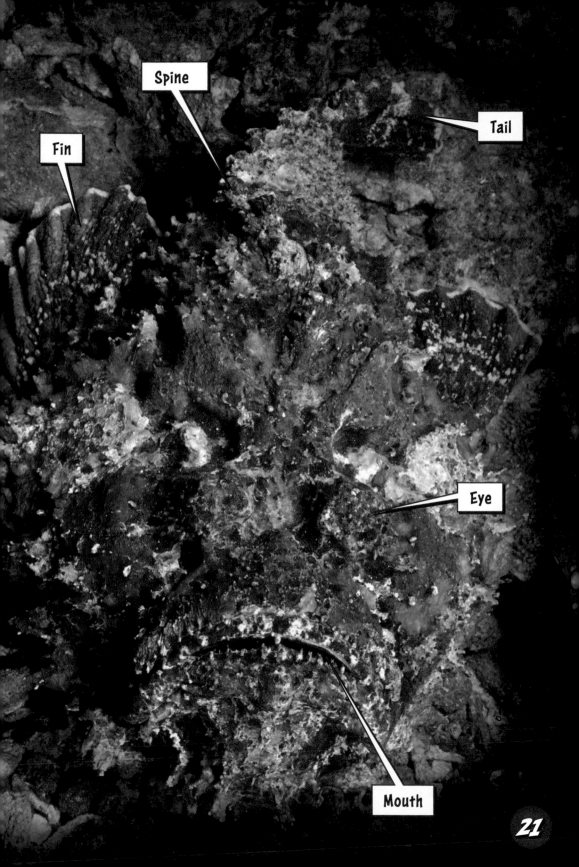

Spine

Tail

Fin

Eye

Mouth

OTHER FISH THAT STING

Stonefish are one kind of fish with a venomous sting. Here are two other kinds of fish that have deadly stings.

LIONFISH

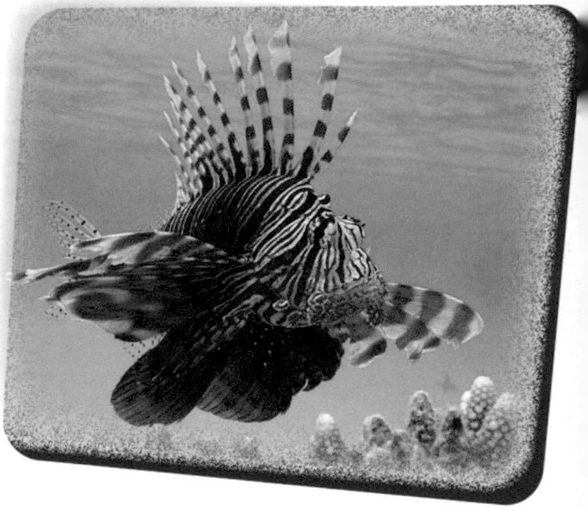

- These colorful fish are found mainly in coral reefs in the shallow, warm waters of the Indian, Pacific, and Atlantic Oceans.
- Lionfish are not usually scared away if something approaches them in the water.
- The fish have long, sharp spines that inject venom.
- Many divers are accidentally injured by lionfish.

STINGRAYS

- These fish are often found in shallow ocean waters.
- A stingray generally has one sharp spine on its tail. The spine injects venom, and the sting is quite painful.

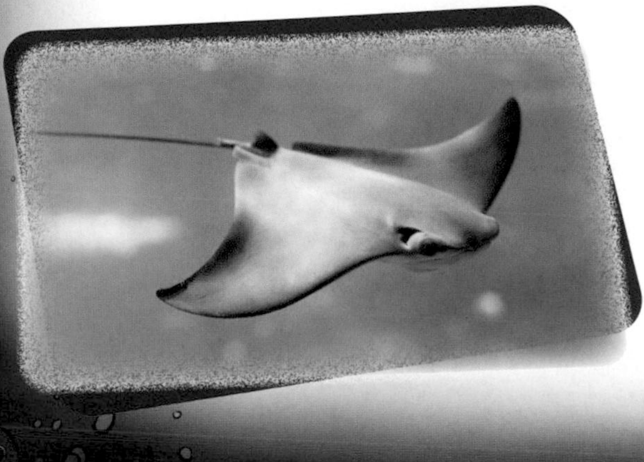

- Stingrays do not attack or sting unless they feel they are in danger or are stepped on.
- Thousands of people are injured by stingrays each year.

GLOSSARY

algae tiny plantlike living things that grow in water

antivenin medicine given to help people bitten or stung by animals with venom

camouflaged hidden or blended in with the surroundings because of coloring or markings on the body

eels long, thin sea creatures

elevated raised up higher than normal

injected pierced with a needlelike object

lunges moves forward quickly and suddenly

polyps tiny sea creatures that live together to form reefs

prey an animal hunted by other animals for food

venom dangerous liquid that flows from some animals that bite or sting

INDEX

READ MORE

Backshall, Steve. *Fish, Squid, and Jellyfish (Deadly Factbook).* New York: Hachette Children's (2014).

Goldish, Meish. *Stonefish: Needles of Pain. (Afraid of the Water).* New York: Bearport Publishing (2010).

Raum, Elizabeth. *Stonefish (Poisonous Animals).* Mankato, MN: Amicus Ink 2016.

LEARN MORE ONLINE

1. Go to **www.factsurfer.com**
2. Enter "**Needles of Pain**" into the search box.
3. Click on the cover of this book to see a list of websites.